Living in

Bangladesh

Written by Ruth Thomson
Photographed by Jenny Matthews

First published in 2003 by
Franklin Watts,
96 Leonard Street,
London EC2A 4XD

Franklin Watts Australia,
45-51 Huntley Street,
Alexandria, NSW 2015

Series editor: Ruth Thomson
Series designer: Edward Kinsey
Additional photographs by Monirul Alam
23(br), Zahidul Karim Salim 8(tl) and
Linda Trew 26(br)
Consultant: Linda Trew

A CIP catalogue record for this book is
available from the British Library.

ISBN 0 7496 5127 X

Printed in Malaysia

Contents

This is Bangladesh

Bangladesh is in southern Asia, bordered by India and Myanmar. Three large rivers, with hundreds of tributaries, flow through the country to the sea. These form the largest delta in the world. Most of the land is flat and less than 10 metres above sea level. The only hills are in the north and south-east. Tigers still roam the dense, swampy forest of the Sundarbans, in the south-west.

△Tea growing
Tea is grown on the hills around Sylhet. This area is cooler and has more rainfall than the rest of Bangladesh.

Fact Box

Capital: Dhaka
Population: 133 million
Official language: Bangla (Bengali)
Main religions: Islam (83%), Hinduism (16%), Buddhism and Christianity (1%)
Highest mountain: Keokradong (1,230 m)
Longest river: Surma-Meghna (669 km)
Biggest cities: Dhaka, Chittagong, Kulna, Rajshahi
Currency: Taka

△**Memorial statues**
Bangladesh was once East Pakistan. These statues commemorate the founding of Bangladesh in 1971.

▷**Crops**
The soil is extremely rich. The main crop is rice. Others are jute, wheat and vegetables.

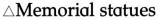

4

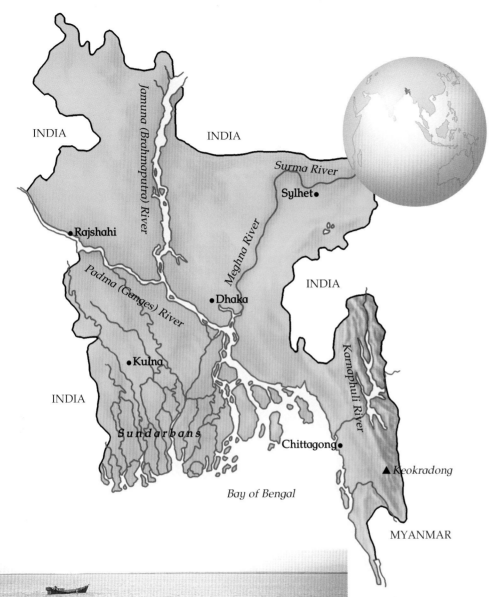

◁**The coast**
The southern coastline
is almost 600 km long.
It is broken up by numerous
rivers flowing into the sea.

△**The population**
Bangladesh is
the most crowded
country in the
world.

5

A land of rivers

The Padma and Jamuna rivers that flow through Bangladesh start in the Himalaya mountains in India. In late spring, these rivers swell with melted snow and flood the land. This yearly event makes Bangladesh's soil rich and fertile. However, summer monsoon rains and cyclones can often turn the flooding into a disaster, washing away homes and crops and killing people.

△**Flooded land**
When the rivers flood, they dump a new layer of rich soil, called alluvium, on to the land.

▷**High rainfall**
More than 2,500 mm of rain falls each year. Most of it falls during the monsoon, between June and October.

△**Living by the sea**
People who live on the coast earn a living either fishing, harvesting salt or farming shrimps. They are most at risk from cyclones.

> ▷**A cyclone shelter**
> Strong concrete shelters are built high off the ground. They keep hundreds of people safe during a fierce cyclone.

▽**Rice fields**
Raised banks of earth surround the rice fields. These trap water inside the fields, so that the rice can sprout underwater.

△**Water supplies**
Children enjoy the plentiful water supplies but they must be careful after the monsoon as the water is often polluted.

◁**Long-stalked rice**
Bangladeshis grow long-stalked rice. The grains ripen in the sun above the floodwaters.

7

Religion

The star and crescent of Islam

More than four out of five Bangladeshis are Muslim. The rest are Hindu, Christian or Buddhist. Every community has a mosque, where Muslims pray together. Mosques have a prayer room and an area for washing. Often, there is also a *minaret* (tower), where a *muezzin* (crier) calls people to prayer five times a day.

△At the mosque

Friday is a holy day for Muslims. Men meet at the mosque for midday prayers and to hear a sermon. They leave their shoes at the door as a sign of respect.

◁Prayer time

This man is rolling out mats at a mosque, for people to kneel on when they pray.

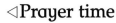

△**Daily prayers**
Women and girls mainly pray at home. They always face in the direction of Mecca, the birthplace of Muhammad.

▽**A Hindu priest**
This is a Hindu priest. He cares for the temple where Hindus go to make offerings to images of their gods.

◁**Ramadan**
During the holy month of Ramadan, Muslims do not eat or drink in the day. At sundown they break their fast with something sweet.

△**The Qu'ran**
Muslim boys go to mosques to learn to read the Qu'ran (the sacred book of Islam). They cover their heads with a *topee*.

Dhaka – the capital

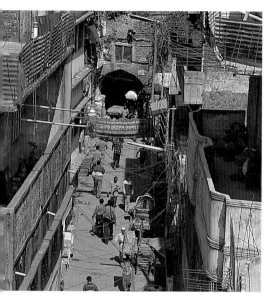

A view of a street in old Dhaka

Dhaka is the capital of Bangladesh and the biggest city in the country. It has two parts – an old and a new city. The old city is a maze of narrow, winding lanes with old houses and shops. The new city has wide roads lined with modern flats and shops, high-rise offices, the university, several parks and the huge National Stadium.

△**The new city**
Most people in the new city live in flats, although there are also some houses with large gardens.

▷**On the river**
The river running through the city is always busy with ferries, cargo ships, tugs, rowing boats and motor boats.

◁ **National Assemby**
Members of Parliament
meet in this modern
concrete building.
It is built in the shape
of a lotus flower.

IT ZONE
Cyber Cafe
PER HOUR 15 TK @ 9am to 3pm
PER HOUR 20 TK @ 3 to 11pm
NET 2 PHONE
CD WRITING/COMPOSING
93/A Bashiruddin Road Kalabagan,
Dhaka -1205, Tel: 018-270829

△**City traffic**
The number of cars is
increasing every year.
There are long traffic
jams, especially at
rush hours.

*An internet
café sign in
the city centre*

▷**Air pollution**
The air is polluted with
traffic fumes and brick
dust from building sites.
Traffic police wear
masks for protection.

Living in cities

Fewer than one in seven Bangladeshis live in cities. However, the size of cities is growing, as thousands of people from the countryside arrive every year, hoping to find work. Most industries are in cities. There is a steel mill and oil refinery in Chittagong, which is also a busy port. More than a million people work in clothes factories in Dhaka or Chittagong.

△New housing
There is a building boom in high-rise flats. These will house better-off city dwellers.

△City jobs
Unskilled rural people may find work as labourers or as bicycle rickshaw drivers.

◁A shopping mall
In recent years, several air-conditioned shopping malls have been built in Dhaka.

△Electricity supplies

The demand for electricity is growing all the time. Cities cannot always supply enough, so there are often power cuts.

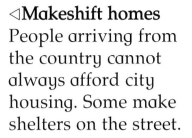

◁Makeshift homes

People arriving from the country cannot always afford city housing. Some make shelters on the street.

△Baby taxis

In order to reduce air pollution, new baby taxis run on clean, compressed natural gas (CNG).

◁Water pumps

Those who do not have running water at home collect water from pumps in the street.

△Bicycle rickshaws

Bicycle rickshaw drivers attract customers with their brightly decorated vehicles.

Living in the country

Most Bangladeshis live in small villages in the countryside. Since almost all the land in Bangladesh is suitable for farming, villages are scattered throughout the country. People build their houses on the highest available land.

△**Village houses**
Houses are usually made of mud bricks, with thatched or corrugated iron roofs.

△**A water pump**
Tube wells provide clean water from deep underground.

▷**Walking**
Villagers rarely own cars. They may walk many kilometres a day, carrying heavy loads.

14

△A village shop
The village shop sells basic goods, such as soap, matches and salt.

◁A pot seller
Travelling salesmen walk from village to village, selling their goods.

▽River fishing
Villagers living near rivers catch fish in the early morning before tending their crops.

Many villages are near a river. Riverside houses are often built on stilts. Mud embankments protect homes and crops from flooding. Irrigation canals leading from rivers supply water to fields during the dry season.

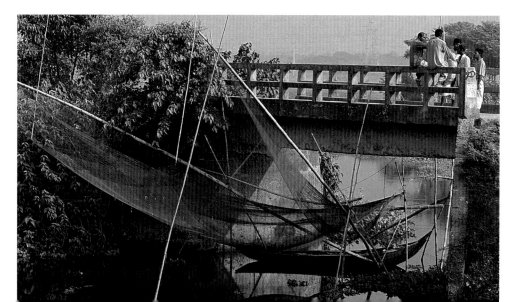

Working in the country

Most people work on the land. Some have their own small plots. They grow rice, pulses and vegetables for their families. Wealthy landlords (*zamindars*) own most of the land. They pay landless people to plant and harvest their crops. Some landless people farm a *zamindar's* land and give him part of their harvest as rent.

△Tea picking
Tea is an important crop. Workers pluck only the top two leaves from the sprigs of each bush.

▷A tea factory
Tea leaves are left to wither and then broken to release their juices. They are laid out to ferment and later dried. They turn dark brown or black.

△Rice growing
Farmers can grow two crops of rice a year. The main crop is planted in June and harvested in December.

16

△**A weaver**
In some areas, women set up wooden looms at home and weave their own cloth.

Some of a farm's vegetable crops

Radishes

White pumpkin

Aubergines

Cauliflower

Beans

Green chillis

Red chillis

△**A goldsmith**
Skilled craftspeople work at home or in a workshop. This man makes gold jewellery.

Some people earn money as craftsmen or labourers, or go abroad to work. People with neither skills nor land can find it difficult to feed their families. Organisations, such as the Grameen Bank, lend money to small groups of villagers, so they can work together to earn a living.

△**Brick breaking**
Bangladesh has hardly any stone. People smash bricks into bits to use as hardcore.

△**At the airport**
Many men with no land or job fly to the Middle East to work. They send money home.

Shopping

Shops are mainly small and run by a single shopkeeper. There are also traders who set up roadside stalls or wander about selling their goods. In cities, people can shop for clothes and household goods in markets, called *bazars*.

△**Live chickens**
Few people have fridges. People buy chickens live and kill them at home, so the meat is fresh.

△**A food shop**
Only some foods are sold pre-packed. Shopkeepers measure out rice, pulses and other dry foods from large sacks.

◁**Neem sticks**
This man is selling neem sticks, which many people use for cleaning their teeth.

Bangladeshi bank notes and a stamp

▽A supermarket

There are a few supermarkets in Dhaka. Much of the food they sell is imported and expensive. Only the well-off shop here.

△Food shopping

People shop for fresh fruit and vegetables in open-air markets. Bangladesh recently banned the use of plastic bags. Now, people use shopping bags made of jute or paper instead.

△A bicycle shop

Bangladesh makes its own bicycles. These are a popular way to get about in such a flat country.

On the move

In a country criss-crossed by more than 700 rivers, boats are far more important than road or rail transport. In the wet season, road journeys are particularly slow, as the heavy rain makes many roads very muddy.

△**A passenger ferry**
Small ferries carry passengers up, down and across the bigger rivers.

△**Lorry ferries**
Big ferries transport lorries across wide rivers where there are no bridges.

A lorry painted with bright patterns and pictures

◁**Buses**
It is quite usual for passengers to travel on the roof of buses as well as inside.

△City transport
People travel around towns and cities in bicycle rickshaws, baby taxis or buses.

△Carrying the harvest home
After the harvest, farmers carry their crops home on poles, slung across their shoulder, like this.

▷Delivering goods
Lorries are banned from Dhaka during the day. Goods are delivered on carts pulled by hand or bike.

Men carrying their shopping home from market

Family life

Most people live in close-knit, extended families. When a woman marries, she moves in with her husband's family. This might include his parents, his brothers and their wives. Women rarely used to work outside the home, but this is now changing, especially in cities.

△**Tribal family**
There are about 20 different tribal groups in Bangladesh. Each has its own distinct customs, beliefs and way of life.

△**Family roles**
Women often marry at a young age. They generally stay at home, preparing food and caring for children.

▷**Family size**
The average number of children per family has dropped from 6 to 3 in the last 30 years. Families are bigger in the country than in cities.

A father taking his daughter to school

◁**Wood collecting**
It is often the
children's task
to collect wood
for cooking fuel.

▽**Child care**
Older girls look after their
younger brothers and sisters.

△**Selling in the street**
Boys sell snacks, drinks and
flowers in the street.

In most families in Bangladesh, it is
essential for children to help out.
In towns and cities, boys often earn
money to help improve the family
income. In the country, boys help
in the rice fields or tend the farm
animals. Girls help with cooking
and cleaning chores at home.

△**Stone breaking**
In some families,
children help with
their parents' job, such
as stone breaking.

23

Time to eat

Rice, pulses and vegetables are the staple foods for most Bangladeshis. A typical everyday meal at home consists of boiled rice with spicy lentils and a meat or vegetable curry (*masala*).

Roadside food stalls sell cheap, filling snacks and drinks, such as sweet, milky tea (*chai*) and fresh coconut milk.

A selection of fresh vegetables in a market

▷**A restaurant meal**
A restaurant meal usually consists of several dishes served in separate small metal bowls. Other typical dishes include roti bread and chicken khorma.

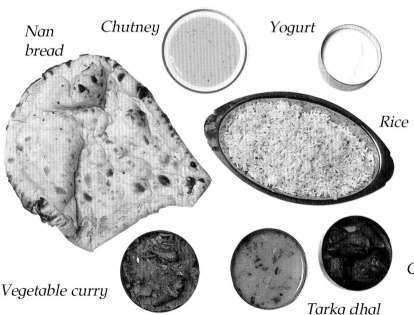

Nan bread
Chutney
Yogurt
Rice
Vegetable curry
Tarka dhal
Chicken tikka

△**Fish**
Fresh fish is cheap and forms a main part of many people's everyday diet, as fish curry.

Pan, a mouth freshener, is eaten at the end of a meal.

△Fast food
Western-style fast food restaurants have recently opened in Dhaka.

△Snacks
Popular snacks include freshly-cooked hot dishes, breads and pastries.

▷ *Tiffin* delivery
Many women make lunch for their husbands. They put the food in a stack of metal containers, called a *tiffin*. Boys deliver the *tiffins* to the men's workplace.

School time

△**A school bus**
Some children travel to school in a bus pulled by a bicycle.

Bangladeshis value education, but not everyone has the chance to go to school. Government primary schools are free and open to all children. However, poor families find it hard to survive without their children working. So, only seven out of ten children start primary school, mostly boys. Children usually go to school for three or four hours a day, except Fridays.

△**A private nursery**
Well-off families can send their children, from the age of three, to fee-paying nurseries.

△**A tea estate school**
Tea estates have their own schools, which children of tea workers attend.

△**A government school**
The government provides books and equipment for children in primary schools.

◁Secondary school

Boys and girls go to separate
secondary schools,
which are found
only in cities
and towns.

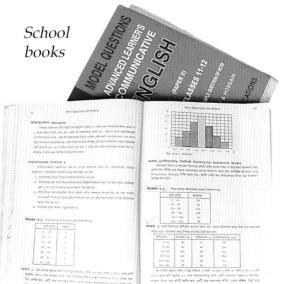

*School
books*

△Literacy

Only half the men and a third of
women in Bangladesh can read
and write. The most
highly educated group are
middle-class boys.

▷Higher education

Bangladesh has more than 15
universities and colleges. Dhaka
University, founded in 1921, is
the oldest.

Having fun

Weddings and festivals (*melas*) are colourful events that everyone enjoys. Some of the festivals mark the start of a new season, when people cook particular dishes and wear new clothes. Everyday fun includes swimming in rivers and playing cricket and board games.

△ *Karam*
These children are playing *Karam*, a board game where players have to skilfully flick counters.

▷ **Cricket**
Cricket is a popular sport. The national team competes in international events. Only men go to watch the matches.

△ **Chess**
Players often set up a game of chess in the street. A group of spectators may eagerly follow it.

△In the park
The bigger cities have parks where people come to stroll and picnic. The parks often have boating lakes.

▷Satellite TV
The most popular programmes on TV are Indian films and cricket matches.

△A country funfair
Travelling fairs, with rides like this one, visit even the remotest villages.

Going further

The royal Bengal tiger

About 400 large tigers are believed to live in the dense forests of the Sundarbans, in south-west Bangladesh.

Find out about the life and habits of these tigers (see www.enchantedlearning.com or www.planetark.org). Create a tiger-faced shaped booklet about the tigers.

Rickshaw art

Bicycle rickshaws are decorated all over with brightly coloured designs. Painters include eye-catching images of movie stars, sun-sets over dreamy landscapes and scenes of modern life.

Imagine you have been asked to decorate a rickshaw. Design a bold and colourful Bangladeshi scene for it.

Embroidery

In parts of Bangladesh it is a tradition for women to make embroidered quilts (*nakshi kantha*) for their children. These used to be made from layers of worn-out clothes, stitched together with patterns and pictures. Some are now made of cotton.

Invent your own quilt design, using dotted lines, like these embroidery stitches.

Websites

www.virtualbangladesh.com
www.greenbangla.com

Glossary

Border The boundary that separates one country from another.

Currency The money used in a country.

Cyclone A fierce tropical wind that forms at sea and blows into land in a spiral, bringing heavy rain. It often causes huge tidal waves on the coast.

Delta An area of land at the mouth of a river, formed by a build-up of soil and sand washed down by the river. These drop to the river bed when the river slows down as it nears the sea.

Embankment An artifically raised riverbank made to prevent flooding.

Hardcore Loose stones and other rubble used as the foundation underneath paved roads.

Irrigation A system of watering farmland, often by digging canals and ditches.

Jute A plant native to east India. The long, tough golden fibres of its leaves are used for making sacks, rugs, bags, mats and hammocks.

Literacy Being able to read and write.

Monsoon Seasonal winds which change direction from one time of year to another. In south-east Asia, the monsoon blowing in from the Indian Ocean brings heavy rains.

Polluted Damaged by chemicals, fumes or other waste products.

Population The number of people who live in one place.

Pulses The edible seeds of certain plants, such as lentils, peas and beans.

Slum An area of unplanned and overcrowded city housing, with no power, water supply, sewers or rubbish collection.

Staple A food that people eat every day.

Tributary A small river or stream that flows into a larger river.

Index

© Aladdin Books Ltd 2005

Designed and produced by
Aladdin Books Ltd
2/3 Fitzroy Mews
London W1T 6DF

First published in
Great Britain in 2005 by
Franklin Watts
96 Leonard Street
London EC2A 4XD

ISBN 0 7496 6272 7

Editor: Katie Harker
Design: Flick, Book Design
and Graphics
Illustrators: Q2A Creative

The author, Dr Bryson Gore, is a
freelance lecturer and science
demonstrator, working with the
Royal Institution and other
science centres in the UK.

A catalogue record for this
book is available from the
British Library.

Printed in Malaysia

Picture research: Alexa Brown, Katie
Harker, Flick Smith, Nick Whittaker

Photocredits: l-left, r-right, b-bottom, t-top,
c-centre, m-middle. Front cover c, 10-11 –
Michael Mueller/Ingram Publishing/Q2A. Front
cover bl, 5bm, 18-19 – Digital Stock. 1m,
16-17 – Photodisc. 2-3, 12-13, 12tr, 29, 31 –
Digital Vision. 4bl, 24-25 – Digital Stock/Q2A.
4br, 6-7 – Q2A. 5t, 28 – Corbis. 5tm, 14-15 –
RogerSteene/imagequestmarine.com/© Mary
Lou Frost. 5m, 22-23 – Corbis/Q2A. 5b, 26-27
– Tony Waterer/Digital Vision/Q2A. 7br – Flick
Smith. 8br, 9 – Ingram Publishing. 9bl – John
Robinson. 10m – © Linda Gettmann. 14b –
Michael Abrams. 17mr – NOAA Photo Library.
20-21, 30 – C F Gottfried/Monarcha A C.
22br – Corel. 25b – US Fish & Wildlife Service.

Introduction

Humans have practised BIOLOGY – the study of all the living things that inhabit our world – for hundreds of thousands of years. In what ways are we the same as other animals and in what ways are we different? How did the species that we see on Earth today come into being? In the last 200 years, scientists have studied these and other questions that help us to understand how life works.

In ancient times, people all over the world looked for ways to explain how all the different forms of life on Earth came into being. Different cultures chose different explanations for creation, but at that time no one considered an idea that has now become central to the modern scientific explanation of life – evolution.

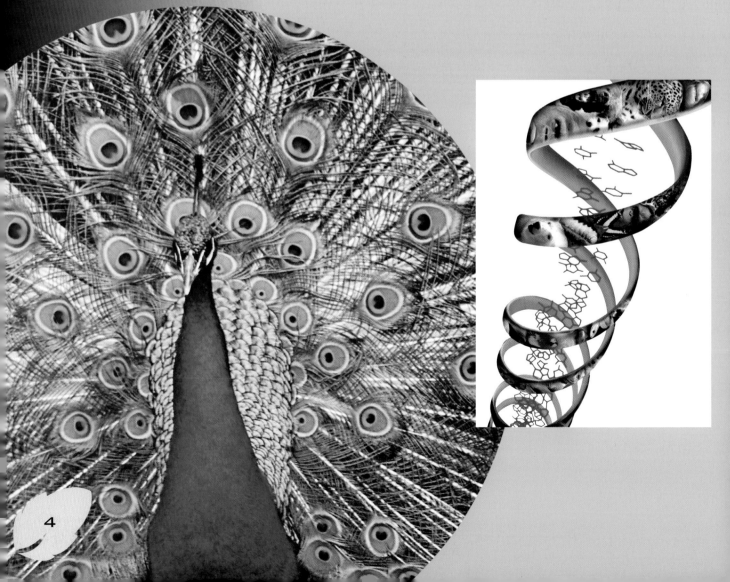

About two hundred years ago, biologists began to discuss how evolution could occur. As scientists investigated the age of the Earth, they came to realise that life has existed on Earth for millions of generations. Fossil records also show that species have changed dramatically over that time.

Biologists like Darwin and Mendel studied the living creatures in the world around them and saw that inheritance was a key factor in reproduction. The inheritance of genes passes common characteristics to future generations, but we can also see that animals are generally suited to the environment in which they live. Today, we understand that many species – living high and low, in heat and cold – have actually adapted to their environment by evolving. But now the world is changing faster than it has for thousands of years. We don't know how quickly animal species can adapt to this change, or whether we are actually entering the latest in a long history of mass extinctions.

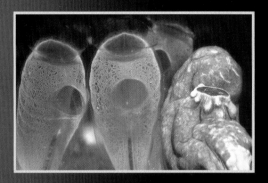

This book takes a look at twelve of the most amazing biological discoveries that have taken place through history. Find out more about famous scientists like Crick, Franklin, Watson and Wilkins and learn how they used their skills to make sense of the genetic code. By consulting fact boxes such as 'The science of...' and 'How do we know?' you will begin to understand more about the ways in which we have pieced together the story of animals, species and life. Learn about genetics, evolution and the amazing skills and feats of the animal kingdom.

How do we know?

Two great scientists opened our eyes to how, over millions of years, evolution has developed all the species of animals that we see today. In the 19th century, Gregor Mendel was an Austrian monk who studied heredity. Mendel looked at the characteristics of pea plants (such as how tall the plants grew and the colour of their flowers), and realised that plants were passing on information about their characteristics in some form of code. We now refer to this as a 'genetic code'. Today, scientists have studied heredity in thousands of different species of animals and plants. They have found that all living things use DNA (deoxyribonucleic acid) to pass on their genetic code. DNA is an incredibly long spiral molecule that controls how cells behave. Parents pass some of their characteristics to their offspring through copies of their DNA.

At around the same time, the English scientist Charles Darwin undertook a five-year sailing expedition. When Darwin studied the living things around him he realised that animals of one species remain similar to each other as they breed, but occasionally minor changes occur. Over thousands of generations those changes can add up in a population to enable it to adapt to change or even create a new species.

ALL ANIMALS ARE DESCENDED FROM A SINGLE SPECIES

The Earth today is home to billions of different species of animals, plants and bacteria. But scientists now believe that all life has a common origin and that every living creature on Earth is descended from a single species that lived thousands of millions of years ago.

Humans are an example of a single species of animals; so are cats, crocodiles, canaries and cobras. Where did all these different animals come from, and what is it that makes one species different from another?

Biologists know about the history of life on Earth from fossils (right) – traces of an organism embedded and preserved in rocks. Fossils show us that, over millions of years, species appeared, disappeared and slowly changed. This process is called 'evolution' and means that any two species on Earth today must have had a common ancestor at some time in the past.

Scientists believe that all animals evolved from a single, very simple, species of animal that lived about 700 million years ago. Biologists estimate that this would have been a tiny worm-like creature that absorbed and digested single-celled organisms from the water around them. It is thought that the offspring of that species evolved into every species of animal that is alive on Earth today.

7

ALL MAMMALS LIVE FOR ABOUT ONE BILLION HEARTBEATS

Mammals make up a single group of animal species and have many things in common, such as their skeletons and the way in which they give birth and rear their young. Scientists now realise that mammals also live, on average, for almost exactly the same number of heartbeats!

Electrocardiograms (below) are used to record the regularity of heartbeats.

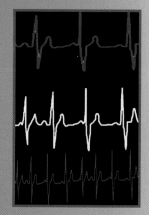

HOW DO WE KNOW?

The most important thing that all mammals have in common is that they all feed milk to their young. This milk is produced in 'mammary' glands that only mammals have. Unlike most animals, mammals are 'warm-blooded' and by maintaining their body at a steady temperature, mammals enable chemical reactions to occur more efficiently within their body. This does mean, however, that they need to eat extra food to keep warm. Mammals also have hair (or fur) to act as insulation. Other groups of species use scales (e.g. reptiles) or feathers (e.g. birds).

The skeletons of many animals are similar, but all mammals have exactly the same number of bones. It's not hard to imagine that the skeleton of a dog and an elephant are similar, but it's more surprising, perhaps, to know that giraffes have the same number of bones in their necks as humans and mice!

All mammalian hearts pump blood to the lungs and then around the body using four separate chambers. Although the heart of a mouse is thousands of times smaller than the heart of a whale, apart from size, they are almost identical! We now understand that mammals have common features because they have kept certain characteristics during evolution.

THE SCIENCE OF...

When you look at all animals in the world, it's easy to see how different they are. But scientists often find patterns to these differences, indicating close relations between species.

Mice have very fast heartbeats (about 300 beats per minute) compared to an elephant (about 50 beats per minute). Mice live for just a few years, whereas elephants live for about 50 years. But, if you calculate how many times their hearts beat in their lifetime, it comes to about 1,000 million (1 billion) for both species! Although this is only a rough guide, the same calculation for other mammals tends to come to the same number. Except for one species – humans! Our natural heartbeat is about 60 beats per minute which means that we would 'expect' to live for about 45 years. A few thousand years ago this was probably an average human lifetime, but civilisation and science have helped to increase average lifetimes to almost double that today. Although exercise raises your heartbeat, don't worry – it's not using up your life! Exercise keeps the heart healthy, lowers your regular heartbeat and increases your chances of a longer life.

9

SPIDER SILK IS STRONGER THAN STEEL

Humans have developed some of the most sophisticated materials in the world. Steel for building giant skyscrapers, Kevlar for stopping bullets and drugs to cure illnesses. But nature has evolved substances that rival anything that we've invented. From spiders to cuttlefish shells, nature's engineers still have a lot to teach us.

THE SCIENCE OF...

Spiders make different types of silk for different purposes. When spiders spin a web to catch their food they use a sticky silk that can stretch without breaking, entangling their prey as it struggles in the web. Drag line silk is the 'safety line' that all spiders have when they move around from different surfaces. This stronger silk supports the weight of their body and is also used for the 'spokes' of a web. We now know that drag line silk is stronger than steel.

The cuttlefish (right) is a marine animal related to octopuses and squids. Although cuttlefish are invertebrates, they keep their shape and protect their internal organs with a single 'bone'. Cuttlefish move from the surface of the ocean to enormous depths and usually this variation in water pressure would crush an animal's skeleton. However, a cuttlefish bone has a special structure – it is made from millions of tiny boxes, each less than a millimetre across. The cuttlefish fills these chambers with gas in the same way that a submarine pumps air into its buoyancy tanks. However, for its weight, the cuttlefish is more efficient than a modern submarine at keeping afloat.

HOW DO WE KNOW?

The animal kingdom is full of creatures that produce materials to suit their needs. The key to natural materials is their structure at cellular level. Although we cannot control the production of synthetic materials with this kind of microscopic detail, we have learnt how to use natural systems (living cells) to manufacture new products based on nature's design.

Silk is one natural fibre that is farmed on a massive scale. Over 100,000 tonnes of silk are produced each year from the cocoons of silk worm caterpillars. Each cocoon is made from a single fibre which can be almost a kilometre long! Winding several of these silk fibres together produces a single thread of silk.

Experiments have shown that spider silk is stronger than steel of the same thickness. For this reason, scientists have attempted to farm spider silk for commercial use. They have been confronted with difficulties though – spiders need space to live and they also tend to fight each other if they are crowded together! However, in 2000, scientists announced a new approach to spider silk collection. By successfully transferring the DNA for spider silk into the genetic code of goats, they enabled female goats to produce spider silk protein in their milk. Goats can produce up to 10 grammes of spider silk protein in their milk every day – thousands of times more than the largest spider!

A N ANT CAN LIFT 50 TIMES ITS OWN WEIGHT

Could you lift yourself off the ground? Do you think you could lift two of your friends up at the same time? Could you lift 50? Small creatures like ants and fleas can perform tasks that we find amazing – but when we come to understand the science, it's not really a miracle.

THE SCIENCE OF...

The world record for weight-lifting by a human is over 200 kg. That's about the equivalent of lifting three people, but in comparison to some members of the animal world that's puny! Ants can lift up to 50 times their own weight and the rhinoceros beetle can carry over 500 times its own weight. Fleas are only a few millimetres tall and yet they can jump up to 300 mm into the air. That's nearly 100 times their size! But these amazing feats are not unusual in the world of mini beasts.

We now realise that being small can make life a lot easier for an animal. In order to get around, every animal needs to be able to lift itself against the force of gravity. As animals get bigger this becomes more and more difficult. The largest creature alive on Earth today is the blue whale (above). Because the blue whale lives in the sea, the water supports its weight – of around 100 tonnes. The largest land creature is the elephant. Biologists now realise that the leg bones of any animal much bigger than an elephant would be unable to support its weight. It is now estimated that over half of the animals on Earth are too small to be seen with the naked eye. But what gives tiny animals such an advantage in the world?

How do we know?

There are many advantages to being a mini beast. Firstly, all the really big animals that might eat you find it hard to see you! If you are small, the food that you eat and air that you breathe also have less far to travel to all the cells in your body. It's a fact that big animals are stronger than small ones. But how would we expect the strength of an animal to vary with its size? Let's imagine three animals – a cat, a cow and an elephant – and suppose that their sizes differ to approximately a power of ten. If the bones of each of these animals changes in proportion to their overall size, the elephant is about ten times longer, ten times taller and ten times wider than the cow. That means that it's 1,000 (10x10x10) times heavier. But its leg bones would only be about 100 (10x10) times stronger because changing the length of the bone does not increase its strength. As animals get smaller their strength relative to their environment increases enormously. Elephants can't jump without injuring themselves. This means that you, a flea and even a mouse can jump higher than an elephant can.

AN ADULT SEA SQUIRT EATS ITS OWN BRAIN

Why do almost all animals have brains but plants do not? Scientists now believe that it's because animals move around. To co-ordinate sensors (eyes, ears and touch) and the muscles that allow us to move, the body requires a central processing unit – the brain. To test this theory, scientists looked at an animal that doesn't move and found a perfect example in the sea squirt!

YOUNG SEA SQUIRT

THE SCIENCE OF...

The sea squirt is an unusual animal. It starts life as a microscopic egg that floats freely in the sea. Over a few weeks the egg develops into a larva – a small creature that resembles a tadpole, with a head, tail and, most importantly, a simple brain that runs along its tail and controls the larva's swimming movements. However, when the larva finds a suitable rock surface, it attaches itself and begins to grow into something that resembles a plant as it is washed by the waves. The sea squirt pumps seawater along its tube-like body to filter out food and releases waste products into the sea, but because it no longer needs its brain to move, the brain slowly shrinks away and is reabsorbed into the body.

Some plants, like the venus fly trap (below), move their leaves or seed pods when touched. When an insect lands on a venus fly trap it disturbs 'trigger hairs' which cause the leaves to close around the insect. The plant then releases chemicals that help it to digest its food. Although the venus fly trap can recognise prey as opposed to inanimate objects, these are purely mechanical processes. Plants do not need to have a brain or a nervous system like animals.

HOW DO WE KNOW?

When an animal moves, it needs to co-ordinate the movement of different parts of its body in order to move efficiently and to avoid unforeseen dangers. Simple animals have just a few hundred connected nerves that enable different parts of the organism to communicate very quickly and to co-ordinate simple reflex movements. Higher animals have hundreds of millions of nerve cells shared between a spinal cord, to provide long-range communication, and a brain where the nerve signals are processed. Nerve cells need to travel from the spinal cord to the end of the arms or legs to stimulate muscles and transmit the sense of touch to the brain. In larger animals, this means that a nerve cell can be several metres in length! The cell body has long fibres coming from it.

Biologists now realise that the size of a brain is not the key to how powerful it is. By studying the fossils of early human species, we know that human brains used to be about 20 per cent bigger than today. However, our brains have become more complex with more connections – this appears to be one of the keys to intelligence.

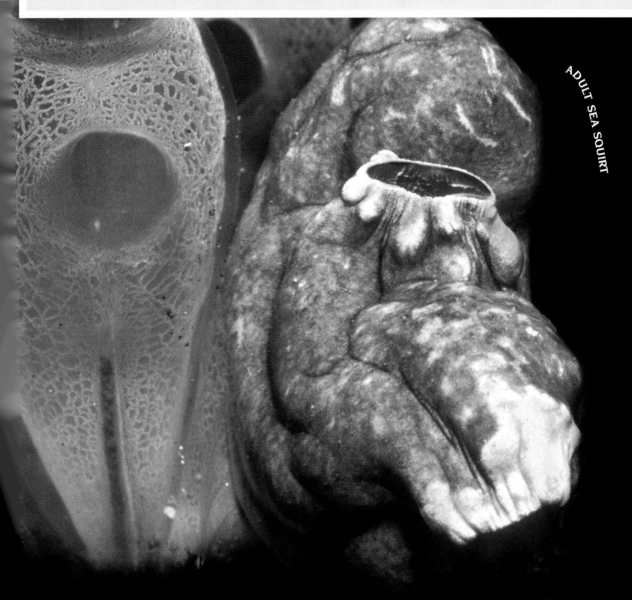

ADULT SEA SQUIRT

15

CRABS HAVE THEIR SKELETONS ON THE OUTSIDE

Humans have a skeleton to keep their shape and to protect vital organs like the brain and heart. Our skeleton is on the inside, but did you know that some species have their skeleton on the outside? It's called an exoskeleton.

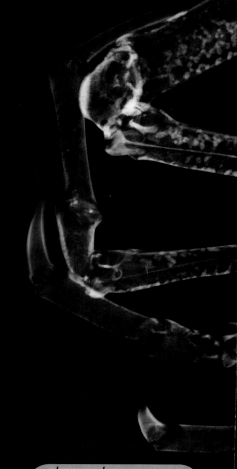

HOW DO WE KNOW?

Plants don't have any need for a skeleton. Instead, water pressure within their cells – aided by stiff cell walls – creates a type of 'hydrostatic' skeleton that acts as a support.

The animal world is split into two halves – those that have a skeleton and those that don't. We call these 'vertebrates' and 'invertebrates'. Of the 10-20 million species that are alive on Earth today, roughly 99 per cent are invertebrates!

The bones of all mammals are made from a material called calcium phosphate. Bones can be incredibly strong. A human thigh bone (femur) can support the weight of several tonnes. Many animals also use cartilage – a mixture of protein and long chain sugar molecules – for support. Cartilage also helps to protect the ends of bones where they meet and rub together. Without cartilage the ends of your bones would rub away as you moved around.

Crustacea and insects do not have internal skeletons but cover the outside of their bodies with a hard shell called an 'exoskeleton'. Exoskeletons are made from chitin – a long chain sugar molecule that is quite similar to the cellulose that stiffens the cell walls of plants. Chitin is shed and replaced as the animal grows.

WOWZSAT!

ALMOST ALL FOSSILS SHOW THE REMAINS OF AN ANIMAL'S SKELETON. THE FLESH AND OTHER SOFT PARTS ROT AWAY BEFORE THE FOSSIL FORMS. THIS IS WHY SCIENTISTS ARE STILL UNSURE WHETHER SOME DINOSAURS HAD FUR, FEATHERS OR SCALES.

THE SCIENCE OF...

As an organism becomes more complex it becomes increasingly important that the different parts of the body stay in the right place and are protected from damage.

The animal kingdom has evolved three main ways to achieve this. The first is for an animal to simply fill itself with water at relatively high pressure – a hydrostatic skeleton. This is how slugs, jellyfish (right) and most small animals keep their shape. Larger animals have hard internal or external skeletons that are part of the animal's intrinsic design.

A skeleton provides a set of levers that muscles can use to exert forces to move around. The arms, legs, wings and flippers of many animals use bones in this way. Bones like the skull and rib cage also help to keep organs in their correct positions and protect them from damage. Insects, spiders and crustacea (like crabs and lobsters) have their skeleton on the outside. This provides great protection but makes movement more complicated.

17

How do we know?

All animals need to take in oxygen in order to stay alive. Mammals, reptiles and birds have lungs that inhale air containing oxygen and exhale air containing carbon dioxide – a waste product from their body's cells. Insects and crustacea do not have lungs but instead have tiny tubes, called 'trachea', that allow air to get to different parts of the body. Trachea are not as effective as lungs and this is why insects cannot grow to be as large as most mammals and birds.

Mammals that live in water have to come to the surface to breathe air into their lungs. Fish and sharks do not have lungs. Instead they have 'gills' that absorb oxygen as water flows through them. There is about 30 times less oxygen in water than air, so gills have to work hard! Fish can pump water through their gills (though most sharks cannot), by drawing in water through the mouth and forcing it through the gill cavity. If a fish stops moving through the water it can still pump water through its gills to stay alive.

Do sharks sleep? Scientists are not really sure! It seems that sharks are able to keep swimming while different parts of their brains 'switch off' in turn. But because sharks never rest entirely they have to eat far more than other fish of a similar size. This is partly why sharks have got such a reputation for being big eaters!

WOWZSAT!
SOME SHARKS CHEAT BY WEDGING THEMSELVES INTO CAVES THAT HAVE A STEADY CURRENT FLOWING THROUGH THEM. BY LETTING WATER FLOW OVER THEIR GILLS, THE SHARKS TAKE A REST AND LEAVE THE WATER TO DO ALL THE HARD WORK FOR THEM!

SHARKS HAVE TO KEEP SWIMMING IN ORDER TO STAY ALIVE

It's easy to think that sharks are like other fish, but they're not! Sharks are amongst the oldest species alive on Earth today and are different from most fish in a number of important ways. Sharks are heavier than water – and this means that they have to keep moving to avoid sinking!

THE SCIENCE OF...

Sharks have existed on Earth for over 450 million years. But the species has done well to survive that long – if sharks stop swimming they sink, and if they stop moving altogether they drown!

Fish have evolved from a species that had a special organ in its body called a swim bladder – a small bag filled with air, rather like the buoyancy tanks of a submarine. This allows the fish to adjust its weight to match that of the water around it. Thanks to the swim bladder, a fish can go to sleep and safely remain at a constant depth.

Other types of sea animals do not have swim bladders and find that life underwater is more difficult. Mammals like whales and dolphins have lungs that are full of air so they naturally float to the surface. This means that they need to swim against their own buoyancy to find food in the depths of the ocean, and also need to come to the surface to breathe. Sharks are heavy creatures but they have evolved ways of reducing their body weight. Their skeletons are made from cartilage instead of bone and they have a lot of fat in their bodies to help them to float.

MONARCH BUTTERFLIES MIGRATE OVER SEVERAL GENERATIONS

Many animals spend their entire lives in one place while others are forced to migrate every year as the climate changes from summer to winter. Monarch butterflies fly from Mexico to the United States and back every year, but when each butterfly lives for a maximum of six months, how do they find their way home?

THE SCIENCE OF...

Monarch butterflies are amongst the most remarkable migrators known in nature. In Mexico, during the winter months, millions of them cover the trees like leaves, but in spring they take flight and head north to the United States or as far as Canada. Monarch butterflies usually live for just over a month, but during the migrating season they can stay alive for up to six months. The 'mature' butterflies reproduce before they die and their offspring make the journey south to Mexico again. The incredible feat of these butterflies is that the next generation (or their offspring) return to the same valleys that their ancestors left behind!

European eels also migrate but their journey lasts a whole lifetime. Eels born an ocean region called the Sargasso Sea in the Atlantic, travel to Europe on the ocean currents. When they reach the European coast they swim upriver and live for 10 to 20 years before swimming thousands of kilometres back to the Sargasso Sea to breed and die. All of these amazing feats are believed to be guided by remarkable senses of smell that identify routes and locations by the chemicals they contain. The butterflies do not know where they are going, but they are 'guided' by their senses.

HOW DO WE KNOW?

Many species migrate. You have probably seen birds collecting in large numbers in the autumn as they get ready to fly to warmer climates.

The migration of the monarch butterflies is monitored by amateurs and professional scientists every year. As the butterflies are spotted, they are reported to a central organisation that charts their progress north. Migrating monarchs can also be tagged and recorded along their journey. Records show that the butterflies can travel over 1,500 km.

Tagging has also been used to follow the migration of birds. Traditionally, birds were tagged with a ring on their leg. If recaptured, a bird could be identified and its movement recorded. Today some animals, like salmon, are tagged by electronic transmitters. These allow scientists to keep a far more accurate measurement of their migration. Large groups of birds can also be monitored with a type of radar that is usually used to track aeroplanes. When birds migrate in flocks they reflect enough radio waves to be seen on radar screens. Radar has been used to monitor flocks of birds travelling over thousands of kilometres.

Migration records are now beginning to show that migrating patterns are changing quite dramatically. A disruption to the environment, caused by humans, is believed to be the central reason, although the importance of pollution and global warming are not yet fully understood.

A FLYING EAGLE CAN SEE ITS PREY FROM OVER 5 KM AWAY

Birds of prey have eyes that outperform all other animals in terms of detail at long range. But did you know that many other animals have specialised eyesight too – insects and snakes can see colours that mammals can't see and octopuses have eyes that are designed to produce a very clear image.

THE SCIENCE OF...

Of all the senses that animals have evolved, the eye is probably the most useful and powerful. Scientists now believe that species have developed similar visual abilities independently, because of the advantage that visual awareness brings.

There are three main types of eye in the animal world. Eyes similar to our own are found in all vertebrates, like mammals, birds and snakes. Insects have compound eyes that use many hundreds of very simple eyes collected together to produce an image. Cephalopods (octopuses, squid and cuttlefish) have eyes that are similar to our own but the nerves and blood vessels of the eye grow around the eye and do not impair vision (see page 23).

Almost all animals have two eyes because this enables the brain to judge distances more accurately. Animals that are hunted (prey) usually have their eyes widely spaced so that they can spot an attack from any direction. Hunters (right) usually have their eyes close together so that they can make an accurate estimate of where their prey is. Birds of prey have the sharpest vision in the animal kingdom.

How do we know?

Eyes are a great advantage to any animal. Even without a lens, if light-detecting cells are in a depression on the body (e.g. an eye socket), shadows can indicate where light is coming from. If the depression becomes covered with clear skin and the cavity (an eyeball) fills with water, it creates a simple lens that improves the image produced on the back of the eye (retina). Vertebrate eyes suffer from one major drawback – the blood vessels that supply the eye and the nerve cells that take signals to the brain grow 'into' the eye and leave via a region near the back called the 'blind spot'. One of the simplest eyes in nature is found in snakes. Pit vipers have normal reptilian eyes but they also have depressions, or pits, along their lower jaw. At the bottom of the pits are cells that can detect the infra-red light, or heat, given off by warm-blooded animals. These eyes help to locate prey in dark conditions.

WOWZAT!

BIRDS OF PREY HAVE OVER 100,000 LIGHT DETECTING CELLS PER SQUARE MILLIMETRE ON THE BACK OF EACH EYE. THAT'S MORE THAN TEN TIMES AS MANY AS HUMANS HAVE. THIS ENABLES BIRDS OF PREY TO DETECT FINE DETAIL IN A SUPERIOR WAY TO OTHER MAMMALS.

HOW DO WE KNOW?

The key to a peacock's ability to predict rain is its sense of hearing. Sound is a vibration in the air around us. Humans hear a limited range of pitch (or frequency) of sound – from about 20 to 20,000 waves per second. Bats hear up to 100,000 waves per second, and peacocks and other birds can hear sounds as low as 0.2 waves per second. Storms emit very low-pitched sounds that can travel long distances. When birds hear bad weather coming they seek shelter.

Birds can also detect the magnetic field of the Earth and this is the supersense that can assist homing pigeons and migrating birds. Sharks are able to detect the electric field that surrounds all living creatures and use that to locate their prey in dark or muddy conditions.

The first animal that was shown to detect ultraviolet light was the ant. Sir John Lubbock experimented by shining different coloured lights onto ants. Red light brought no reaction, green or blue light encouraged the ants to repair their nest and ultraviolet light encouraged the ants move their pupae back into areas of darkness. Biologists now recognise that many insects and birds can see colours beyond the range of mammals.

PEACOCKS CAN PREDICT RAIN

For thousands of years it has been known that birds like peacocks can predict the coming of storms. Other birds can navigate on cloudy nights and many animals react to natural disasters, like earthquakes, long before humans become aware of the impending disaster. These animals seem to have senses that we do not possess. Biologists call these 'supersenses'.

THE SCIENCE OF...

The animal world is full of creatures that need to detect the world around them in order to find food and to avoid danger. Mammals have five senses, much like our own – touch, taste, hearing, smell and sight. However, many mammals have finer senses of touch, hearing and smell than we do. Dogs are particularly good at detecting scents, and bats (below) can locate a flying insect in complete darkness.

More distant species of animals have more advanced and completely different senses. Insects and birds are guided to the location of nectar on many plants by colours that the human eye cannot see. Migrating birds travel thousands of kilometres and recover from being blown off course by storms. Homing pigeons can find their way back from places they have never been in pitch black conditions. Sharks and electric eels are able to detect their prey to far greater accuracy than could be explained by sound or vision alone. Biologists are beginning to understand how many of these marvels are performed by studying the senses and supersenses of the animal world.

MOST SPECIES ON EARTH DISAPPEARED AT THE SAME TIME AS THE DINOSAURS

Around 65 million years ago, every existing dinosaur species on Earth died out in a period of time too short for us to measure accurately. At the same time, the majority of plant and other animal species on land and in the sea were also made extinct. It was not the first time that such a mass extinction had occurred on planet Earth. So what happened?

THE SCIENCE OF...

The Earth is home to thousands of different animal species today, but in the past other species lived that are no longer alive. Dinosaurs, for example, were the dominant species on Earth for over 150 million years. From the massive Brachiosaurus to the tiny Compsognathus, dinosaurs occupied almost every part of the planet. But around 65 million years ago, an event occurred that killed so many living things that 85 per cent of all species were unable to survive. The species that did survive eventually flourished because there was less competition from other species and evolved into creatures like the ones shown (see main picture). There were no humans on Earth at that time but they, and all species that we see on Earth today, also evolved from the species that survived.

Scientists believe that there have been several mass extinctions during the Earth's history, although the exact number is uncertain. Currently there are six major extinctions that most scientists agree on. They happened about 65, 190, 225, 345, 430 and 500 million years ago. Today biologists realise that thousands more species of animal have died out than are alive on Earth today.

How do we know?

Studying rocks that were formed millions of years ago, and the fossils they contain, is the key to how we can study mass extinctions in the history of the Earth. Scientists believe that at the time of the dinosaurs, a meteorite or comet, 10 km in diameter, collided with the Earth on the coast of what is now Mexico. The energy released was incredibly large – more powerful than a thousand nuclear explosions. Scientists are convinced that the explosion was caused by a rock falling from outer space because they have found iridium deposits in layers of soil deep within the Earth.

Iridium is a metal that is rare on Earth but common in space. Fossils of dinosaurs and other animals are found below the iridium layer, but very few species of animals that used to live on Earth are found in soil above this layer.

Although the mass extinction 65 million years ago was devastating, the largest mass extinction occurred about 225 million years ago. Gases were released by the eruption of massive volcanoes which led to global warming. The increased temperatures and the reduction in the amount of oxygen meant that 90 per cent of marine life and over 70 per cent of land-based species died out.

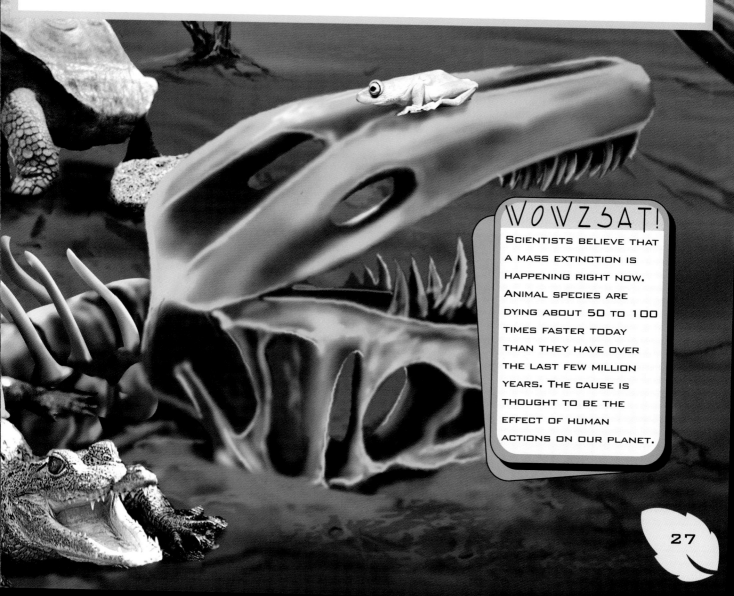

WOWZSAT!

SCIENTISTS BELIEVE THAT A MASS EXTINCTION IS HAPPENING RIGHT NOW. ANIMAL SPECIES ARE DYING ABOUT 50 TO 100 TIMES FASTER TODAY THAN THEY HAVE OVER THE LAST FEW MILLION YEARS. THE CAUSE IS THOUGHT TO BE THE EFFECT OF HUMAN ACTIONS ON OUR PLANET.

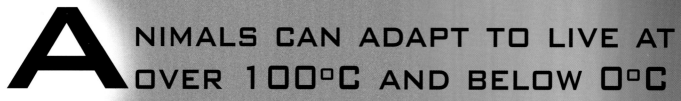

ANIMALS CAN ADAPT TO LIVE AT OVER 100°C AND BELOW 0°C

Animals have adapted to survive the cold of the arctic and the dry heat of the desert by evolving over thousands of generations. But did you know that some animals have even adapted to survive when their body temperatures are colder than ice or hotter than boiling water?

THE SCIENCE OF...

Most animals have adapted to survive in relatively hospitable conditions in or close to water. But as biologists explore more extreme conditions, they find that life is often already there.

The water below the arctic ice is below freezing, yet fish and other animals can survive there. Tiny crustacea, called krill, use oils and fats to prevent the water in their bodies freezing, and several species of fish produce a molecule that is very similar to the anti-freeze that people put into car radiators. This means that they can survive and feed in conditions that would freeze other fish to death.

At the bottom of the deep oceans there are cracks or vents that produce streams of water at over 120°C. Amazingly, although there is no light, biologists have discovered that this water is rich in minerals and is able to 'feed' enormous quantities of bacteria. The bacteria in turn provide food for specially adapted worms that grow to over two metres in length in the waters around the vent. Scientists have found that other animals feed on these worms in a complete and almost isolated ecosystem.

How do we know?

Animals that live in extreme environments have adapted to these conditions by evolving over thousands of generations. In the coldest regions of the Earth, warm-blooded animals, like mammals and birds, use insulation from fur, feathers and fat to maintain their temperature.

Polar bears have adapted to the cold of the arctic with a thick coat of fur and a layer of fat that prevent heat loss. Their white coats also mean that they can move across the snow and catch their food without being seen. Lizards, and other animals that live in the desert, often stay underground during the hottest and coldest parts of the day. Lizards have also evolved long legs to help keep them cool from the hot desert sands. Camels and desert rats have adapted to reabsorb vital water – their noses can retain the water that would be lost during breathing, and they have even developed ways of turning their body fat into water in times of extreme drought.

Evolution is driven by the need to adapt to changing conditions. The Earth's environment has always been changing but in the 21st century, global warming and changes in water supply might happen too fast for many species to adapt.

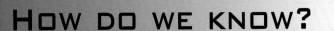

Glossary

Adaptation – The change, over many generations, in a species to suit its environment.

Cartilage – Soft, flexible bone-like material.

Cephalopod – One of a group of species including octopuses and cuttlefish.

Crustacean – One of a group of species including lobsters, crabs and shrimps.

Descendants – All the creatures that inherit genes from a single ancestor.

Digest – To break down food so that it can be absorbed.

DNA (deoxyribonucleic acid) – a molecule that 'stores' the genetic code of living creatures.

Ecosystem – A collection of living things and the environment in which they live.

Electric field – The influence of an electric charge.

Exoskeleton – An external skeleton found in many creatures.

Extinction – The death of every member of a species, or group of species.

Fossil – The preserved remains of a dead animal.

Frequency – The number of waves per second.

Genetic code – The 'instructions' for how to produce the chemicals required for a living creature.

Gills – Organs used by many sea creatures to extract oxygen from water (breathe).

Heredity – The passing on of characteristics from one generation to the next.

Hydrostatic skeleton – A support structure produced by some creatures using water pressure.

Invertebrates – Animals that have no backbone.

Larva – The young form of some creatures.

Magnetic field – The influence of a magnet.

Mammal – A group of species that feed their newborn infants milk.

Migrate – To move from one place to another due to the change of climate every year, or over time.

Molecule – Two or more atoms bonded together.

Organs – A part of a living creature that performs a specific function.

Reflex – An instinctive response to stimulus that requires no thought.

Senses – The methods by which a creature detects its surroundings.

Species – A group of animals that can all breed with each other.

Spinal cord – The extension of the brain that runs within the spinal column.

Supersense – An animal sense that is better or different from the human senses.

Swim bladder – An organ that enables fish to adjust their buoyancy in water.

Trachea – A tube for transporting air within the body of a creature.

Ultraviolet light – Light that is bluer than the human eye can detect.

Vertebrates – Animals with a backbone.

Biography

Walter Alvarez (b. 1940) An American geologist who discovered iridium in rocks about 65 million years old – thought to have been produced by the collision of an asteroid which caused a mass extinction at the time.

Charles Darwin (1809-1882) An English biologist who proposed that natural selection led to evolutionary change.

Sir John Lubbock (1834-1913) An English biologist who studied the behaviour and senses of insects. Lubbock showed that animals can detect colours that humans can't.

Gregor Mendel (1822-1884) An Austrian monk who taught both mathematics and biology. Mendel introduced the idea that characteristics are passed on in what we now call genes.

Francis Crick (1916-2004), Rosalind Franklin (1920-1958), James Watson (b. 1928) and Maurice Wilkins (1916-2004). Four scientists who together worked out the shape and function of DNA (deoxyribonucleic acid). Wilkins and Franklin showed that the molecule was a spiral made up from two separate chains. Crick and Watson worked out how DNA 'stored' and used the genetic code.

KEY DATES

500 BC – Xenophanes studies fossils and proposes a theory of evolution.

350 BC – Aristotle classifies animal species in a series of books.

1660 – Robert Hooke uses a microscope to see animal and plant cells.

1680 – Anton van Leeuwenhoek sees bacteria with a microscope.

1859 – Charles Darwin publishes 'Origin of Species' which sets out his ideas about evolution.

1865 – Gregor Mendel publishes his experiments on pea plants.

1952 – Franklin and Wilkins determine the general structure of DNA.

1953 – Crick and Watson determine the precise structure of DNA.

2001 – The human genetic code (genome) is determined by hundreds of collaborating scientists.

Index